" THE POETRY OF HEARTBREAK "

SHLOK KUMAR

Made with ♥ on the Notion Press Platform
www.notionpress.com

"This book is a portrayal of the relationship between two lovers and their interactions with society, as well as how society perceives them. I've spent several years writing this book to craft meaningful sentences. I hope you'll enjoy reading it."

"Shlok kumar"

Contents

Contents

Preface

Shlok kumar

Shlok Kumar was born in Chadaraha village, Mirzapur district. His parents live in the village, and he completed his primary education there. His mother's name is Rajkumari Devi, and his father's name is Chandrashekhar. His father is a lecturer, and his mother works as a sweeper in the panchayat department. He completed his 10th standard from Shri Ram Public School, Mirzapur, with first-class honors, and his 12th standard from Rajasthan Inter College, Mirzapur, also with first-class honors. After that, he appeared for several central university entrance exams and achieved success in many of them, including Allahabad University, Delhi University, Lucknow University, Rajasthan University, Banaras Hindu University, and Guru Ghasidas University. He also cleared exams like General Nursing and Midwifery, Polytechnic, Engineering, and Rural Technology, National Talent Search Examination, etc. Finally, he took admission in Allahabad University, also known as the Oxford of the East. Currently, he is a third-year student at Allahabad University. His first book, "Hashiye Par Mushar," is based on dalits and casteism. This book changed his life and earned him several awards, including the Asia Book of Records, Delhi Book of Records, Bihar Book of Records, India Book of Records, and World Wide Book of Records. He broke Vicky Kumar's record to become the youngest author to write a book on dalits and casteism. His short story "Jal" secured second place among one lakh participants. He also won first prize in the "A" category of the Woman Hood Fest International Poetry Competition. His

first book is titled "Hashiye Par Mushar," and his second book is titled "Mannat E Alfaz." He writes articles for several renowned newspapers, including JJ News Paper, Ujala Shikhar, Mirzapur News, prayagraj news, and others.

Some of the renowned monthly literary magazines where his poems have been published are:

Pravakta, Anhad Kriti, Sahitya Aaj Kal, Nav Uday, Kavishala, Amar Ujala, My Poetic Side, Hello Poetry, Poetry Soup, Poem Hunter, All Poetry, Submittable.

These magazines and online platforms have featured his poetry, giving him a wider audience and recognition.

"Awards: 'National and International Awards' - Won

- India Book of Records - Won
- Asia Book of Records - Won
- World Wide Book of Records - Won
- India World Record - Won
- Bihar Book of Records - Won
- Delhi Book of Records - Won
- Zakhi Book of Records - Won
- Youth Writer Award - Won
- Golden Book of Records - Won
- Phoenix Book of Records - Won
- Magic Book of Records - Won

- High Range of World Records - Won

- American Book of Records - Won

- Kalam Book of Records - Won

- Marvelous Book of Records - Won

- Extraordinary World Record - Won

Nominated for:

- Youth Icon of India

- Bharat Youth Award

- Guinness World Records Excellence Award"

1. " A traumatic old man "

Oh! my beloved
Without thou I am like a dud man in this rangy world.
Mine condition is like a beggar without a goblet ,
Like a flower without fragrance,
Like a body without chromatin,
Oh! dear God forgive me,
And return my beloved to this sombre life of mine.
My time travel is becoming arid, bittersweet.
Day by day I am getting numb,
It feels like mine whole body has become paralysed without her.
Oh ! Oh ! Cruel God
Account mine love,
Why don't thou understand mine anguish, I don't know how to live without her,
In mine unabridged life I have only learnt to love stogy and her,
I have forgotten what is the eventual purpose of mine life?
Send her into my soul and aloof me from this insidious world.
My soul is in anguish more than that azoic bird,
I got it in a moment by the ruth of gosh, allah.

Send my soul with mine beloved to empyrean, where we
will offer thou a rosary of flowers with
our blood, our pain, our tears.
Don't chasten me with that bloody whip, cruel God,
My only audacity was that I loved her
My soul is in agony, have ruth on me
Listen to the screams of my beloved, the voice of her soul
You will hear her helplessness, the voice of her dissociation
from mine.
I am scared in this murk room, thine Janitor are appal me
with their screams,
Let me hear just one breath of mine beloved,
Have ruth on this child of gosh,
I want to plosive her before I die,
My pious tears are now quirking into black tears.
Mine breathing is getting heavy, my heart beats are
becoming fast
I don't need any treatment,
Give me her breath, her fragrance, her heartbeats of life.
Return my beloved on mine last journey.
The blinking of my blepharon is vindication mine every
breath,
Murk is making its home in these eyes,
Mine breaths still sensate thou,
O brutal butcher God,
Have ruth on me now.
The emblem of whip are reviving mine amour,

Every emblem is pleading for her,
Mine body is being torn into pieces by this agony,
Now you come, my beloved come back.
A vox was heard nervy in the room,
I was slumbering next to my beloved,
And abruptly the author kissed his beloved,
And hugged her,
Beloved said to him, honey !
don't be afraid, it's just a dream ,
They both kissed each other and started smiling,
And a hurting wound abruptly turned into relief.

Note:- The fantasy is about old man Jack who suffers from separation from his transgender friend Depp. And he is praying to God and his cruel angel not to kill him for his mistakes because he is mindless and sick. You'll read his thoughts and more in this short poem , What Happened to Depp and an Old Traumatized Man. The poem is a powerful expression of love and longing ,with the speaker pouring out their emotions in a passionate and intense plea to be reunited with thier beloved. The use of imagery,metaphor,and other poetic devices adds depth and complexity to the poem, making it rich and rewarding for read.

2. "Holy love"

Spring pass'ed with joy
I'm still waiting thy! My love
Thine dream rubbe'd my wound,
Thine eyes
Faints me every day
Come and confess thy eminence love !
Oh ! My honey don't be late
I'm still waiting thou, at mine's door gate
Spring gone to home,
Autumn about to come ! My love
Lest it happen that I get separated from thou like that pale leaf,
Catch me ! My honey
Oh ! My love come and come
And confess mine divine love
Shut the broken heart's
and be like ocean
don't see the krishna's contrastic flute's
whose sound faint everyone's,
see only mine's divine love
oh ! my love, accept mine love and be heaven's of Queen
my heaven's queen,

let us drown in our sacred love
and acquaint world's with this newness raise of love.
Note:- This poem is dedicated to my beloved who took too long to understand my love. Who has been separated from me because of some lie and the lover is trying to convince his beloved. Spring came and went but could not bridge those distances. Autumn is about to come and the poet is saying, my dear. I should not get separated from you like that yellow leaf, hold me and accept my love, this poem creates a contradiction between spring and autumn.After reading this poem, you will feel that the author is convincing his beloved but he is convincing his classmate by giving false praises and telling about his great love for her. The characters in this short poem are Shlok Kumar himself and his classmate Sneha Singh Narendra.This poem has been written on 26 February 2024.

3. " Dream:- My Honey "

O! O! O! Joyful day
Why thou feel mine sorrow today ?
Mine time travell is not going better
Don't feel mine soul bitter
Oh ! Oh ! Joyful day,
Don't be so rude with mine
I don't have wine
to forgot mine sorrowness.
Oh ! Close friend be polite
I know , thou have great day light
O ! My lady
let's go for swum in eden lake
Sink with mine,
Forget the sorrow day
and forget the way
Oh ! Oh ! My lady
Forget the bitter day.
Just sink in mine inner soul
there's nothing way to come out
Oh ! Honey don't shout
It's just dream
got up and see around

Oh ! Oh ! My honey
how darling thou're ?

Note:- This dreamary poem defines lady Julie's desire. She want to do swum with her lover at eden lake . Julie's lover is an author who sat on the freely and comfortable chair and writing, he felt that Juli is dreaming but he don't disturb her, he wants to make Julie dream better to not contract her dream with her emotions. It's just fictional poem which he wrote with Julie's dream.This poem is written on March 5, 2024.

The poem is a melancholic and introspective piece that explores the theme of sorrow and longing. The speaker is addressing a joyful day, but ironically, they're feeling sorrowful. They express their emotional pain and bitterness, seeking escape from their troubles.

The poem takes a romantic turn when the speaker invites their lady to join them for a swim in Eden Lake, symbolizing a paradise or haven. They urge their lady to forget their sorrow and sink into their inner soul.

The tone of the poem shifts abruptly when the speaker awakens from their dream, addressing their honey with affection. The poem concludes on a tender note, highlighting the contrast between the speaker's sorrow and their loving relationship.

4. " Lover's like a cover "

Nowadays mine past , haunting mine too much,
i don't know , Why ?
But it's generated my love for her again,
Oh ! Gosh don't do such type of vast fault,
She forgot our love
and She is now with other.
Perhaps,mine soul is thinking more
she has many faces and hearts
which she easily wore.
Oh ! Oh ! My poor past
don't be stick with mine
I'm not glass of whisky wine
O! My cheater lady
come and do account of our love ,
it's been for mine tough
stop thine hallucinations and fake love
it's enough.
Oh ! Oh ! Oh ! Wind , Sky, planet
please justice with mine
order her to don't call or
don't chant fake love tune.
Because, she destroyed mine whole life and love too ruin

Order ! Order ! Order !
Oh ! Cruel wind
justice with poor lover
I'm just a useless love cover.

Note:- This poem is about the author's beloved who has moved on with her new lover. But the author still has feelings for her and her past haunts him but the author doesn't want to be with her again. His girlfriend Julie, whom the poet loved very much, was a very beautiful and thick-haired young girl. For a time she also loved the poet very much but Julie's love faded with time. During their separation, the poet sought an account from those winds, clouds and planets in front of which both of them had sworn never to be separated.This poem is written on March 7, 2024.

5. " My love , My life "

On a morning day, i arose
felt like dreaming and
i kiss thou thrice,
forehead, lips, eyes.
Oh ! My sweest lady
don't blink
just connect the love link.
Forget the divine love and gosh also,
let's go with mine,
I'll probably give great love than them,
O! O! My honey,
don't chant fake love
just end the love chapter with mine,
It's taken time to forgot bitter love,
accept my pure love and got freedom wave.
Don't chase mine in outer world,
just be with mine dream,
otherwise I'll kiss thou and
bind with mine life long couple ,
Don't regret, don't think, don't hesitate
Kiss mine with thee blossom lips,
And feel like heaven's queen.

Aww ! My loveliest lady
slept with thou and felt like got heaven,
touch thou felt like got something,
hugged tightly thou felt like got everything,
Kissed thou felt like got juicy taste,
thine body smells, like
rose,
After having with thy,
Mine felt like got success, long life , love , everything.

Note :- This poem is about the author's beloved who has moved on with her new lover. But the author still has feelings for her and her past haunts him but the author doesn't want to be with her again. His girlfriend Julie, whom the poet loved very much, was a very beautiful and thick-haired young girl. For a time she also loved the poet very much but Julie's love faded with time. During their separation, the poet sought an account from those winds, clouds and planets in front of which both of them had sworn never to be separated.This poem is written on March 7, 2024.

6. " O! My Mind "

Partition with thou my love !
Mine mind converting into hell day by day,
Seems nothing way to over out from that hell.
O ! Lord take mine at thine feet.
I'm tire to see myself,
It's all about intense shit,
least sex worker wimin
too better than mine and mine fuck mind ,
Mine mind like human's stool,
Which's Fully pack with nuisance thought,
Felts regret without any matter.
Oh ! Gosh pour some wine from heaven,
I drank and forgot the thoughtless world
and became like play boy ,
Who always Chirp ,
When need Sexual pleasure.
Oh ! Oh ! Oh ! My mind
it's all about mine intense shit
Oh ! Gosh take mine at thine feet
and vanish mine nudity mind with thy holy bless.
I'm fucking shit man , wants always sexual pleasure,
oh ! oh ! oh ! My mind

it's not gentleman's intense
Be like gentle , be like follower of gosh
O ! Fucking mind
be like pure wind
and spread good thoughts around thine,
Stop the sexual imaginary
be like gentleman,
thou'll got the life's victory.
Oh ! Oh ! Oh ! Shit mind
sing the chant of god ,
quit that wrong path,
It's moment pleasure not more than that ,
and moment pleasure enough to destroy thy whole life.

Note:- This contradiction romantic poem is written by Shlok Kumar 4 February 2024, The author is talking about his idle days when he realized that his mind was turning sensual and that idle mind was filled with sexual thoughts. He felt that it was not according to his ability. And how to overcome those thoughts and sexual pleasure that he feels like doing but does not want to do those things. Sometimes we don't want to do such a stupid thing, but we are at this age like an immature and teenager, it is actually not our fault, This is simply due to the sex hormone testosterone.

7. " My near lady , thine long hair "

Oh ! My thick long hair lady,
Thine hair smell's like rose
but when i started to write it's interrupt mine ,
I'm helpless, emotionless, because of better smell,
Oh ! Long hair
if thou attract mine towards thy ,
how i'll console my heart, emotion,
just vanish mine attachment
with thine love lotion.
Oh ! My hand want's to write
but thy hair disturb mine hand like polite.
Oh ! Living hair don't make mine fall in love thy,
I'm attached towards thine but pack of shy.
Thine lady boss chide on thou,
to not cut the joke with shy boy
But thou're mad with towards on mine ,
Oh ! thick long hair
just stick with mine like cocktail of wine,
O ! O ! My queen's of life
Just see once , I'm whispered alone

Thou're mine broken heart soul
Just see once again my queen of life,
How I survived without thine ?
Oh ! Oh ! Oh ! My lady
Listen to mine ,
just see me and forgot everything,
Aww! Aww ! My long thick hair lady ,
Just attach and died with mine ,
Nothing have special in this selfish world,
Cut the heart with knife neck's round.
Oh! Oh! thine immortal hair just hug mine
and feel the lucidity of thine attachment,
I'm dead and be state of unconscious mind,
Oh ! sorrowful wind just blow and mixup mine into
beloved thick hair.

Note:- This imaginary poem is written on Kumar's imagination based on his class. When the author is giving his yearly examination then a girl who is sat infront of kumar and her thick long hair is distracting him many times. Her long hair smell like flowers of blossom and seems like a bunch of garlands. It's is time of march 18, 2024 , when Kumar is traveling by train.

8. " O ! My butcher lady "

My heart pumps like as thou emotion's
Seems like mine heart slaver of thine,
Oh! My love come fast
thy country's far threescore mile.
Don't be habitual of thine for mine,
how'll survive i Without thou?
My lady, came and fill
mine broken heart,
with thy eminence love,
I'm feeling like mine heart a vacant desert.
Thy promises frustrate mine ,
it sounds again and again of thee fake's promise,
She said to me that thou're bloody fool,
Thou feel like that i gives importance to thee,
but thou're like human's stool.
Oh ! Oh ! Oh ! Gosh
What happened with her ?
She forgot our divine love
She taught me love's chapter
But thy love's chapter
became for mine like slaughter.
She cut mine emotions, love , heart ,

into uncountable pieces,
like She's fond of meat.

Note:- This poem is written on March 6, 2024. Author's beloved is a butcher by profession but he is cheated by her because of some false so kumar is telling about her that she thought his love like meat of chicken's. When she wanted to cheat him, she could that but Kumar wasn't want to separate form her cause of too attachment. This poem is fictional poem which's shows a beloved and lover love for eachother other and shows loyalty, false promises, accusations.

9. " Aww ! Quit the bloody knife "

Aww ! Aww ! Gosh
What happened to them ?
everyone's become like butcher,
found every single town a cruel butcher
they calle'd its their profession
if human's said animal's body profession
then cut thine body's too
and spread double profession.
Oh ! Oh ! isn't this the new modern society
Where human's mad to
cut animal's useless body,
and trying to double their money.
Oh ! Cruel Human
be a holy saint.
be vegetarian and be merciful ,
like a good human
otherwise thou're kille'd by nature like monster,
Oh ! Oh ! Gosh
Boy cut chicken's meat ,
father cut human's feet ,

Noone's alive without did bull shit.
It's spread like disease all over the world,
Each and each person unescaped without any penalty,
Gosh come on the earth
and do account them ,
and pour out cruelty.
teach them mankind, leniency,
make them a proper human being,
thine fear ended as seeing.
O ! O ! Cruel butcher
don't be like devil
thou're human have thine emotions ,
have also family,
don't be thought thine're Hitler
Thou knows very well ,
what's happened with butcher Hitler
He committed suicide by his gun,
same like one day thou'll cut thine neck by knife.
O ! Butcher
Let drown thine knife,
Be like sky's star.
twinkle like great lighter.

Note:- Aww ! Nowadays person convert into butcher form and call it's their profession. To satisfy their families satisfaction and need by cutting animal's body. If is this profession then do double earn by cutting their own family's body. Kumar is strictly against to this human's disease and said it's not profession of their, it's instant please for them to feel bloody hand , bloody mentality. There's nothing benefits for their family to do this work but they're helpless with their bloody mind and nothing to control on them. This sorrow poem is based on the real incident place of Kachhawa meat market, Aslam Ahmad a 18 year old boy converted into butcher by his father.He never regret to do this because he thought it's his destination. And he cut chicken's meat so fondly and happily. Perhaps he satisfied to do this but he'll accounted in heaven by lord.And it's depend on his work to go for heaven or hell.

10. " Don't Chant, help the needy "

O ! Gosh ,art thou in human's body ?
or just it's only proverbs,
because if thou art in human's body,
then stop human's propaganda that they identified himself as gosh,
because thou art one, and no other copy of thine in this world,
if to talk to thine, I need to any saint or prophet then i relinquish to chant or love thee,
if I've purity , innocency, kindness, then thou'll accept mine into thine feet without query,
if a criminal or thief, woman beater , violence man relinquish their path and confess thine crime infront of thine,
then thou'll also confess their pray ,
Oh ! My lord , my goodness lord
Stop ! Stop !
Dirty people's propoganda
who wants to call himself as fake gosh,
it can get people's harm

poor people who doesn't educate ,
they'll get robbed by fake chanter,
Fake chant like bow , chanters like arrow,
they'll shot silently by giving gosh order,
Fie ! Fie ! Dirty propaganda
it's all about their selfish,
stop thine business
and confess thine crime into gosh court,
Stop ! Stop ! really stop nuisance merchant.

Note:- Shlok Kumar told about his village mentality in this poem, how they're treat people and cheat them by using god name for money and fake esteem.Kumar's mother is too religious and pure heart lady. who belief on chanting but it's not her fault it's just environment and impact of society's old lady.Kumar is also religious but he's totally against to show off and fake believe.This poem was written on March 20, 2024.

11. " O ! My worthy pen "

O ! My worthy pen
don't be stuck in world's hallucinations
Just flow ink with mine mind all around,
Fille'd world with smell of love,
Repair the broken heart wound.
O ! O ! O ! My loveable pen
be always with mine ,
Never be separated or
don't fall in love with other,
thou're mine first love,
if thou cheated with mine
I'll do thine murder.
O ! O ! My worthy friend
thou helpe'd me a lot
with thy effort, hard work
with thine great ability
when everyone had left mine,
Thou're only one,
who stood with great capacity and unity.
O! My inkless pen

thou didn't stop, just relaxed on the way
Come and again flowe'd the words flood,
and fille'd human's body with great knowledge,
Flow thy word's in human's blood.

Note:- Kumar's pen flowing knowledge and great words all over around.He wants that he never separate with his worthy pen, when kumar faced difficulties in his life then his worthy pen was one and only who stood and be with him . This poem was one of the closest poem of Kumar and this poem written on March 9, 2024. Kumar sat on the corner of the temple and he composed this poem with the help of his useless and unique pen.

12. "A group of Smoker"

Naught's happening just chatter each other,
Mr Rawat talked about the norcotics and Mr Shah just raillery on intoxicated things.
Rawat defined many intoxicated things like drugs, cigarette, nicotine and more.
Seems so habitual and fantastic about the things as he exactly telling about.
they're dined the leaf's of nicotine,
drank the whiskey wine,
No-one conscious about the charmer hell gate,
Whose messanger is still waiting us to deliver the death's speech,
Seeing all these uncommon things, Shocked and consuming human's blood, faint and swing in dream the bloody witch,
It's effect of intoxicated things which is suffering thine mind,
Ah ! Nowadays youngester most of become drug's habitual,
Oh ! Almighty save this young generations youngsters,totally fall in the intoxicated ?
After all the happiness and sadness chattering,

Rawat telling about Gambia place where old lady's buying young, adult and intoxicated people's for a night for her sexual pleasure.

And monthly parceled some allowance to their part time lover , gives apartment also.

Shah commented on this funniest topic, that why should we not try once a great pleasure in the Gambia with black, or white lady,

Immediately says rawat to us , it's, Gosh wish not our. Gosh want to take us in the heavens place so don't deny just accept their guide and rules. Kumar is noticing only on that topic and nodding in the positive way. They reached the Gambia place and enjoyed with Black's, White's old cum young lady. Nowadays generation's youngester start with intoxicated things and end up with sexual pleasure. Kumar, Shah , Rawat drank all the shameless thoughts, activities , and became drugs dealer of Gambia country after taking their experience.

Note:- This essay is written on 8 April 2024 , basically kumar is describing in this essay about the intoxicated things. How kumar created a group of smoker which is his classmates Mr Shah's name is Altmas and Mr Rawat's name is Ranveer Rawat. This is imaginary essay Which contradict to the situation and shows the downfall of human's routine. How They bruised their life with moments pleasure ? Gambia Country is the sex tourist place where young and old men and women comes and got

sexual pleasure with their partners.Some people's give allowance to their Gambia's wife but some people used them for pleasure and left them in hell condition for death. They're also homeless, hopeless, dreamless, jobless so they give sexual therapy with them for survive.At the last they end their life's to taking drugs, and other intoxicated syringe which is affected directly their life and their beautiful body. Basically it's beginning to the intoxicated and sexual happiness and end with their life.

13. Quest for identity

A mother gives birth
while she bears pains,
in trouble too she gives happiness ,
throught her life she never complained .
The only quest was for her identity
where is her place in the society ?
Man is worshipped for manhood
Then why is woman not understood ?
She symbolises modesty ,
She symbolises faith and greatness
She is like a circle axle,
On which rotates the whole society,
Her subjugation would even destroy the nature.
Then only quest was for her identity
Where is her place in the society ?

Note:- This story is written by Shlok kumar the tone of the poem is one of admiration, appreciation, and concern. The speaker expresses a sense of wonder at the mother's ability to endure pain and sacrifice, while also highlighting the injustices and lack of recognition that women face in society. The poem also conveys a sense of urgency and importance, emphasizing the need for women's rights and

recognition.

14. "Beloved's tears"

My imagination has become a cemetery, where tears have become rain.
My heart's restlessness has become a shore, where every wave is helpless without you.
Watching you, I'm killing my own existence, like a sea that's drying up, and tears that have dried up.
I don't know what kind of love you've given me, but every word reminds me of your absence.
The day and night seem like a dark night, and my modesty has become a stain.
The thought of you is making my heart desolate, and your love seems neglectful.
My steps are faltering, and my feet are bleeding, but I don't feel the pain.
My tears are turning into pools of blood, and I'm afraid that this imagination, this pain, might separate us forever.
You're miles away from me, but your memories are still torturing me more than these bleeding feet.
Your love is like a balm that's healing my wounds, but it's also making me cry.
What kind of pain is this, that's sweet and yet hurtful?
Your words are like sharp knives that are reopening my

wounds.
Stop this spectacle of tears, my heart is not willing to listen.
I've lost myself, and there's no one else to blame.
Note:- This poem is a poignant expression of love, longing, and heartache. The speaker's emotions are raw and unbridled, as they pour out their soul in a desperate attempt to convey the depth of their feelings.
The poem is rich in imagery and symbolism, with the speaker's imagination becoming a "cemetery" where "tears have become rain." This powerful metaphor sets the tone for the rest of the poem, which is characterized by a sense of desolation and despair.
The "shore" where "every wave is helpless without you" is another striking image, emphasizing the speaker's sense of isolation and disconnection from their loved one.

15. "The Unheard death"

Why do you sleep in silence, my love?
Tell me your last wish, I implore from above.
Has your memory faded, like the morning dew?
Have you forgotten the ties that bound us, my love, anew?
Why do you gaze upon the path, with eyes so still?
Why do you wait for the call, that beckons you to fulfill?
Were you thirsty for this mortal life, my love?
Were you greedy for this grave, sent from above?
You transcended the heavens, for a fleeting bliss.
Now, you depart, without a kiss. Speak to me, I implore.
In this cursed grave, your peaceful state
Makes me anxious, my heart does await.
What did you desire, my love, in this life?
Was it just a moment's pleasure, or a lifetime's strife?
Why do you look at the path, with eyes so still?
Why do you wait for the call, that beckons you to fulfill?
They say the dead do not speak, but you do say
Something, every moment, in your own sweet way.
Your gentle eyes, your sorrowful face
Do speak to me, in a language of love and grace.
Why do you not speak, my love, and tell me your heart's desire?

Why do you leave me, to burn with love's sweet fire?
O, dear departed, why do you not speak?
Why do you leave me to mourn, with a heart that doth seek?
Your love, your memory, do haunt me still,
And in your silence, I do hear your gentle will.
Why do you gaze upon the path, with eyes so still?
Why do you wait for the call, that beckons you to fulfill?
Why did you give up your life, for that meaningless pyre?
Why did you sacrifice your soul, for that empty desire?
O, dear departed, please don't be so bitter.
Return to me, and let us cherish each other.
Ask the dead about their desires, O river of sorrow.
Why are you in such a hurry, O stream of tomorrow?
Take the colorful ashes of the dead.
Why do you burn the body, and count the moments slow?
Speak to me, I implore, and tell me why you go.
O, dear departed, why do you not speak?

Note:- This poem is a heartfelt and emotional lamentation of a loved one's passing. The speaker is addressing the deceased, asking them why they have left, and why they are not speaking. The poem explores themes of love, loss, grief, and longing. - The speaker is desperate to communicate with the deceased, asking them to speak and reveal their last wishes.

- The poem highlights the pain and longing that follows the loss of a loved one.

- The speaker reflects on the deceased's life, wondering what they desired, and whether they were seeking fleeting pleasures or lifelong fulfillment.
- The poem touches on the idea that the dead may still communicate with the living, albeit in subtle ways.
- The speaker implores the deceased to return, and to cherish the time they had together.
- The poem concludes with a sense of resignation, as the speaker acknowledges that the deceased is truly gone, and that they must come to terms with their loss.

16. "O! Golden time"

O, Golden beloved Time, thou're Not So Special
Thou're not as precious as thy seem,
A mere measure of moments, a fleeting dream.
thy pages turn, a blur of past and present too,
No awareness of time, just a mechanical pursuit.
thy gears tick on, a rhythm so fine,
Yet, no sense of time's passage, no rhyme or chime.
tho're a golden lyre, with strings of silver bright,
But no awareness of time, just a hollow, haunting light.
Tell me, O Golden Time, about thy world so fair,
A realm of wonder, where moments beyond compare.
Doth people wear thou like a badge of honor and might?
Art thou a treasure, coveted, a shining delight?
thy story's one of wonder, a tale of magic and dream,
A world of enchantment, where time's mysteries beam.
But are thou aware of time's passage, its fleeting nature's sway?
Or are you just a measure, a mere mechanical way?
I'm enthralled by your story, O Golden Time, so bright,
A tale of wonder, a world of delight.
But tell mine , doth thou know the value of time's fleeting breath?

Or are thou just a treasure, coveted, yet lacking life's depth?
O, Golden Time, thou're Not So Special,
Just a measure of moments, a fleeting dream to reveal.
thou're not as precious as thou seem,
A mere mechanical pursuit, lacking life's esteem.

Note:- The poem is an ode to time, questioning its value and significance. Time is personified as a golden clock, but the speaker suggests that it's not as precious as it seems. Time is portrayed as a mere measure of moments, a fleeting dream. The poem explores the idea that time is just a mechanical pursuit, lacking life's depth and esteem.

17. " Mother's Affection "

Oh ! My Sorrowful days , Behave with patience and dignity,
In this world, there are two precious words,
Mother and Father, a treasure that's heard.
These words are like wings to a young bird's flight,
Teaching them to soar, and shine with delight.
A mother's love is selfless, a sacrifice so true,
A father's guidance, a shelter, for me and for thou.
They're the first ones we see, when we open our eyes,
And from that moment on, they're our guiding surprise.
In this world, where selfishness reigns,
Parents are the only ones, who love without any gains.
They give up their desires, their dreams, and their youth,
To give us a better life, and a future, of truth.
A mother carries her child, for nine months in her womb,
And gives birth to a new life, with a love that's so pure and so calm.
She nurtures, she cares, and she sacrifices, with a heart so true,
And gives us a life, that's full of love, and full of hue.

But today, in this modern world, we see,
Children neglecting their parents, and their love, so carefree.
They forget, the sacrifices, the love, and the care,
That their parents gave them, without any expectation, or any share.
So let's cherish our parents, and their love so true,
And give them the respect, and the care, that they deserve, anew.
For they're the ones, who gave us life,
And showed us, the meaning, of love, and strife.
I'm grateful for my parents, and their love so true,
And I hope, to make thee proud, and to see them smile, anew.
For they're my guiding light, my shelter, and my friend,
And I'll always cherish, their love, that never ends.

Note:- The poem is a heartfelt tribute to parents and their selfless love. It highlights the importance of parents in our lives, from the moment we are born to the time we grow up. The poem emphasizes that parents are the only ones who love us unconditionally, without expecting anything in return. The poem also touches on the theme of gratitude and appreciation for parents. It encourages readers to cherish their parents and show them respect and care. The poem concludes by expressing the speaker's gratitude for their parents and their love, which is a guiding light and a source of strength.

18. "The Unseen pain"

Oh ! thy're mine beloved ,don't doth such crime ,
thy've intoxicating shine,
It's hurted mine O, my dearest dancer, thou dost bear the weight
Of fate's decree, and wealth's oppressive might.
Endure for a moment, dear dancer, and heed my plea,
Lest thou forget the beauty that thou dost possess, and let it flee.
Thy feet, they move with grace, like petals of a flower,
And in thy dance, thou dost enthrall, with every step, and every hour.
But soft, dear dancer, thou dost bear the scars
Of a world that doth not understand, and doth not care.
Thy anklets, they do jingle, like the sweetest melody,
And in thy dance, thou dost express, the deepest emotions of humanity.
But alas, dear dancer, thou dost face the cruel fate,
Of a world that doth not appreciate, thy beauty, and thy art's estate.
O, fairest dancer, thou dost shine, like a star in the night,
And in thy dance, thou dost ignite, the passion, and the delight.

But soft, dear dancer, thou dost bear the weight,
Of a world that doth not understand, and doth not care, thy plight.
Endure for a moment, dear dancer, and heed my plea,
Lest thou forget the beauty that thou dost possess, and let it flee.
For in thy dance, thou dost express, the deepest emotions of humanity,
And in thy beauty, thou dost shine, like a star, in the vast eternity.

Note :- The poem is a poignant and emotive address to a dancer, highlighting the struggles and hardships she faces in her life. Despite her exceptional beauty and talent, she is not appreciated or valued by the world. The poem emphasizes the weight of societal expectations and the oppressive nature of wealth and power that she must endure.

The poem also touches on the theme of resilience and perseverance, urging the dancer to stay strong and not forget her own beauty and worth. It encourages her to continue dancing as a means of self-expression and as a way to convey the deepest emotions of humanity.

Throughout the poem, the speaker expresses a deep sense of empathy and admiration for the dancer, acknowledging the sacrifices she makes for her art and the impact she has on those who witness her performances.

Ultimately, the poem is a tribute to the dancer's beauty, talent, and resilience, and a powerful exploration of the human spirit's capacity to persevere in the face of adversity.

Note:- The poem is a heartfelt and emotional appeal to a dancer to endure the challenges of life and to never lose sight of their passion and beauty. The poem reminds the dancer that they are a delicate flower in a harsh world, but that they have the strength to rise above the cruelty and scorn of others. The poem encourages the dancer to let the music guide them, to let their spirit soar, and to never forget the beauty that they hold within themselves. The poem also reminds the dancer that they are a star in the night, and that their dance is a beautiful and shining thing. Overall, the poem is a powerful and uplifting message to anyone who has ever felt marginalized, oppressed, or discouraged. It reminds us that we all have the power to rise above our challenges, and to find beauty and strength within ourselves.

19. "Womanhood"

O ! Gosh Woman's special place, a must for progress,
Known to all, through the ages, we've been blessed.
Woman, a symbol of bravery, no longer weak,
But strong and powerful, her spirit unique.
Her story, a testament to her strength,
A tale of courage, in the face of length.
That night, where were thou, when I cried out in pain?
No one came to save mine, from the monsters that stained.
thy bravery, a legend, in the annals of time,
A shining example, of a woman's sublime.
But, oh, the irony, of a freedom that's not free,
A liberty that's tainted, by the stains of humanity.
The government's blind eyes, only see our shame,
Our dreams, shattered and broken, like a mirror's frame.
Manipur, a land of beauty, lost its charm,
A city, once full of life, now lies in alarm.
Listen, oh woman, thou are not weak,
thy strength, a beacon, in the darkest creek.
When did thou become, a symbol of bravery?
When did thou rise, above the ashes of slavery?
Oh, selfish creatures, how dare thou question our right?
A freedom, that's not freedom, but a mere illusion's light.

Take away this false freedom, that's devoid of dignity,
A liberty, that's tainted, by the stains of humanity.
What's the meaning, of a freedom, that's not free?
A liberty, that's lost, in the labyrinth of humanity.

Note:- The poem is a powerful tribute to the strength and resilience of women. It highlights the importance of women's empowerment and progress, and celebrates their bravery and unique spirit. The poem also touches on the themes of freedom, dignity, and humanity, and critiques the societal norms and expectations that have held women back for centuries. The poem begins by acknowledging the special place that women hold in society, and notes that their strength and bravery are a testament to their unique spirit. It then goes on to describe the pain and suffering that women have endured, and asks where the people were when they cried out in pain. The poem also critiques the concept of freedom, noting that it is not truly free when it is tainted by the stains of humanity. It argues that women's freedom is not just about physical liberty, but also about dignity, respect, and equality. Throughout the poem, the speaker urges women to recognize their own strength and resilience, and to demand their rights and dignity. It concludes by asking what the meaning of freedom is, when it is not truly free.

the poem is a powerful call to action, urging women to rise up and demand their rights and dignity. It is a celebration of women's strength and resilience, and a critique of the

societal norms and expectations that have held them back for centuries.

20. “My beloved's boat:-bluff”

Oh ! My beloved,
Take me across, O boatman, to the other shore
Where the ocean’s waves call out, and the winds whisper more
The stormy sea, it beckons me, with its crashing roar
Take me across, O boatman, to the other shore
In the midst of the ocean, I feel the pangs of fear
The waves crash strong, and the winds howl loud and clear
But still I call out, O boatman, take me to the other side
Where the sun shines bright, and the heart can reside
The night is falling, and the stars begin to appear
The ocean’s waves, they whisper secrets, and the winds draw near
The boatman’s song, it echoes through the night
As I journey on, to the other shore, where the light shines bright
I am not afraid, O ocean, of your depths so dark and wide
For I know that I, a traveler, shall reach the other side
My journey’s long, but I shall not tire
For I know that I, a traveler, shall reach the other shore,

where love and peace reside.

Note:- The poem is a beautiful and emotive expression of a person's desire to cross over to the other side of the ocean, both literally and metaphorically. The speaker calls out to the boatman to take them across the stormy sea, despite feeling fear and uncertainty. As the journey progresses, the speaker reflects on the beauty of the ocean and the night sky, and the way the waves and winds whisper secrets and draw near. The boatman's song echoes through the night, guiding the speaker on their journey. Despite the challenges and dangers of the journey, the speaker declares that they are not afraid of the ocean's depths and widths, and that they have faith that they will reach the other side. The poem concludes with the speaker's confidence and determination to reach the other shore, where love and peace reside.

21. "A Lady trapped"

O my honey! these threads have bound mine freedom, mine hands are tied
O, Natwar (dancing lord), release me, give me back to mine beloved
We share a bond, a withered tree, my life is like a branch
Dry and lifeless, I stand helpless, torn apart by thy absence
Mine tears are precious, falling like pearls, O, Natwar, release mine
Don't think these threads are my prison, break them, O, Natwar, set me free
I'm no longer afraid of society, I'm a puppet, a mere plaything
Mine existence is meaningless, O, Natwar, release me
I'm a caged bird, break this prison, O, Natwar, set me free
I beg of you, O, Natwar, release me, I'll give you a penny, just set me free
My heart is restless, without him, my wounds will never heal
O, Natwar, release me, and I'll fill your pockets with gold
Why be a puppet, dear Shlok, why be bound by threads?
His love letters are scattered, torn apart, set them free, O, Natwar, release mine.

Note:- The poem is a heartfelt and emotional plea for freedom and release from the constraints of society and the speaker's own circumstances. The speaker feels trapped and bound by the threads of societal expectations and norms, and longs to be free to follow their own heart and desires. The poem uses imagery and metaphor to convey the speaker's sense of confinement and longing for freedom. The speaker compares themselves to a withered tree, a puppet, and a caged bird, emphasizing their feelings of helplessness and confinement.

Throughout the poem, the speaker addresses Natwar, a figure who seems to hold the power to release the speaker from their bonds. The speaker begs Natwar to release them, offering to give up everything they have in return for their freedom. The poem also touches on the theme of love and longing, as the speaker mentions their beloved and the pain of being separated from them. The poem concludes with a sense of desperation and urgency, as the speaker implores Natwar to release them and set them free.

22. "The Unseen beauty"

Fie ! Fie ! My life Destroyed ,
Days now seem desolate, evenings shrouded in darkness
Mine own mistakes have made me realize, all my dreams have been reduced to ashes
My heart's voice tells me, my existence is but a mere game
Your presence, a fleeting moment, a whispered promise, now but a distant memory
In the moments that feel like eternity, I search for myself
I wander through villages, streets, and cities, but find only despair, deception, and pain
Even thou, it seems, are now deceiving mine, eroding my existence
Like termites, consuming my being, leaving mine hollow
Have mercy on me, I beg of thou, before I perish
Transform me, a humble beggar, and heal my wounds, my torment
When will time, humanity, and circumstances change?
Is this too a momentary phase? Who knows what the future holds?
Is this truth, falsehood, or deception, This era seems like a mere illusion
A fleeting moment, a whispered promise, a distant

memory.

Note:- The poem is a introspective and emotional expression of the speaker's feelings of despair, desperation, and disillusionment. The speaker reflects on how their own mistakes have led to the destruction of their dreams and aspirations. The poem explores themes of existential crisis, self-discovery, and the search for meaning and purpose. The speaker feels lost and disconnected from themselves and the world around them. The poem also touches on the idea of deception and illusion, suggesting that the speaker's perceptions of reality have been distorted by their own mistakes and the influence of others. Throughout the poem, the speaker appeals to an unknown entity, begging for mercy, transformation, and healing. The poem concludes with a sense of uncertainty and ambiguity, leaving the reader wondering about the nature of truth, reality, and the human experience.

23. "Bluff:- The Velvet"

Oh My fainted Whiskey Wine,
thy've shreded waist and shine .
Oh, my love, your intoxicating eyes,
Like lotus flowers, your lips, a treasure to the skies.
Your waist, a velvet lotus, your voice, a cuckoo's call,
Leaves me breathless, and in heaven's thrall.
Show me your mercy, give me your soul,
Take me away from Satan's door, make me whole.
Oh, my love, my goddess, my peace, my heart,
Return to me, give me the bloody wine of heaven's art.
Five decades have passed, yet nothing's changed,
Except the wounds, the heartache, the pain.
I'm dying tonight, show me heaven's sight,
My love, don't be cruel, come back to me, and make it right.
Don't be so harsh with me, my love, it's strange to see,
You're shining bright, but your heart is lost in misery.
Come back to me, let's start anew,
Everything here is temporary, it's all just a view.
Oh, my love, don't create such a colorful world,
This is for courtesans, who sell their beauty for a few coins to unfurl.

You're only interested in colorful pleasures and sex,
But in the end, you'll come with me, and you'll need my love, I expect.
Your body will wither away, your desires will cease,
And in the end, all you'll need is love, a love that brings release.
A love that's not physical, but mental, a love that's kind,
A love that understands joy and sorrow, a love that's one of a kind.
Years have passed, and you're still beautiful, a sight to see,
But you're no longer interested in physical love, it's not for thee.
You're only drinking wine, and smoking cigars, your addiction's grown,
You're helpless, my love, but I'll be waiting for you, alone.
You're dividing your earnings into two parts, one for your addiction, one for your
savings,
This is your daily routine, my love, your life's enslaving.
You're a courtesan, my love, a beauty, a treasure to behold,
But in society's eyes, you're just a sex worker, your life's grown cold.
You wake up in the morning, drunk, and lost, and alone,
In the evening, you sell your body, and count the cost, the pain you've known.
But I know, my love, that you're more than just a shell,
You're a beautiful soul, trapped in a world that's hell.

Your addiction's blinded everyone, but I can see,
The real you, my love, the beauty that's meant to be.
You're a shining star, my love, a light in the night,
A love that's pure, a love that's right.

Note:- This poem expresses a person's deep feelings towards their lover. The poet describes their lover's beauty, charm, and allure, but also highlights their miserable condition and social status. Through the poem, the poet appeals to their lover to change their current lifestyle and improve their life. The poet tries to make their lover understand that the life they are living is destroying them and that they need to change their life. The poet has included various themes in the poem, such as love, beauty, charm, misery, and social status.The language of the poem is beautiful, attractive, and emotional, which attracts readers and helps them understand the meaning and emotions of the poem. This poem is a heartfelt appeal to the lover to change their ways and improve their life, and it highlights the poet's deep feelings and concerns for their lover's well-being.

24. "The sticky Lady"

When noon's warm rays upon my college fell,
My professor spake of fresher's festive spell,
A farewell party, where I was to play
The anchor's role, and guide the merry way..
In BCA's hallowed halls, she did reside,
A sophomore fair, with eyes hid inside,
Her spectacles, a veil to conceal her sight,
Yet laughter danced upon her lips, a wondrous light.
I, senior to her, yet felt awe and fear,
My words, entwined in hesitation's snare,
Her friend, a confident maiden, stood anear,
And with one glance, my courage did unfold and disappear.
"Thy name?" she asked, and I, with humble tone,
Didst whisper low, my heart in tumult thrown,
She bid me join her class, I did decline,
And she, with gentle smile, didst say, "Tomorrow, we shall entwine."
Her presence, a strange, ethereal glow,
Didst fill my soul, and make my heart bestow
A sense of wonder, that I could not define,
As if the world, in her, didst newly shine.

By station's gate, I sought to speak with her,
But she, in whispers, said, "SMS, my dear,
Shall be our medium, till we meet again,"
And I, obedient, didst her words retain.
Days passed, and scarce, our conversations flowed,
Yet, in her voice, my heart didst find a home,
When once she called, and I, in surprise, didst hear
Her tones, that didst my very soul endear.
Her peers didst say, "She's wrathful, odd, and cold,"
But I, in her, didst find a heart of gold,
A river's depth, that didst in silence flow,
And with each word, my love for her didst grow.
"Life," I asked, "what is't?" and she didst say,
"Let all things be, and fade away,
For in the end, 'tis but a fleeting breath,
That we call life, and then, 'tis but death."
Her words, a paradox, of calm and fire,
Didst stir within me, a love most true and dire,
For though her exterior seemed austere and cold,
Her heart, a flame, that didst my soul enfold.
And thus, thou didst capture me,
With words, that didst my heart's deep secrets see,
Thou art not ordinary, but a gem divine,
A maiden, fair, and beautiful, in every line.
Thy reputation, wrongly, doth precede,
For thou, in truth, art gentle, kind, and freed,
From worldly cares, thy spirit doth take flight,

And in thy eyes, a radiant light doth shine so bright.
Though we didst speak but briefly, thou didst steal
My nocturnal rest, and make my heart reveal
Its deepest thoughts, and with each passing day,
My love for thee didst grow, in every way.
Thou art not lost, fair maid, but found,
In every word, and every glance, profound,
Thy words, a balm, that doth my soul revive,
And in thy love, I do find my heart's alive.
Thus, let me cherish every moment we share,
And hold thee close, as my heart's dearest care,
For thou, art a treasure rare,
A jewel, shining bright, beyond compare.

Note:- The poem is a romantic and introspective tribute . The speaker describes how they met in college and were immediately drawn to her unique personality and beauty.Despite initial hesitation and shyness, the speaker found themselves falling deeply in love with a girl . They describe how her words and presence captivated them, and how they found solace and comfort in her company. The poem also touches on the theme of misconceptions and misunderstandings. The speaker notes that reputation precedes her, but that she is, in reality, kind, gentle, and free-spirited. Throughout the poem, the speaker expresses their deep admiration and love for Rishu, describing her as a "gem divine" and a "treasure rare". The poem concludes with the speaker's desire to cherish every

moment they share to hold her close as their heart's dearest care.

25. " A Gambian Julian's Affection "

The story begins with Jack's realization that his life is crumbling. He's addicted to hashish wine, cocktails, wine, and cigars, which have become essential to his existence. He acknowledges his physical decline and dependence on these substances. In his youth, Jack was a strong and wealthy businessman with immense stamina for alcohol and sex. He had two wives: Swan, whom he respected, and Julian, from Gambia, who fulfilled his physical desires. Jack provided Julian with a house and allowance, but with one condition: she could never marry anyone else. Julian tolerated this arrangement but longed for equal respect. When Jack discovered her desires, he became angry and abandoned her, taking away her house and allowance. Julian was left with nothing but her beauty and love for Jack. Years passed, and Swan grew older, eventually divorcing Jack due to his declining health and inability to satisfy her physically. Jack, still addicted and selfish, sought Julian again. Despite Julian's advancing age, Jack didn't recognize him, but Julian immediately recognized Jack. Jack, filled with tears, hugged Julian, but showed no shame

or regret for his past actions. Julian, still blindly in love, continued to support Jack financially and emotionally, despite his continued drunkenness and occasional abuse. Note:- The story revolves around Jack, a wealthy businessman who has hit rock bottom due to his addiction to substances like hashish wine, cocktails, and cigars. He reflects on his physical decline and dependence on these substances. In his youth, Jack was a strong and wealthy individual with a high stamina for alcohol and sex. He had two wives, Swan and Julian, whom he treated differently. While he respected Swan, he objectified Julian, providing her with material comforts but denying her respect and equality. When Jack abandoned Julian, she was left with nothing. Years later, after his divorce from Swan, Jack sought out Julian again, still addicted and selfish. Despite his past wrongdoings, Julian continued to support Jack financially and emotionally, blind to his flaws and still deeply in love with him. The story explores themes of addiction, objectification, and the complexities of human relationships, highlighting the destructive nature of Jack's actions and the enduring power of Julian's love.

26. “A Baredi:- Untold Pain”

A shepherd’s life, a daily grind
With animals by his side, he walks in line
His heart is like a river, flowing free
But his life is one of toil, with no liberty
He’s a brave man, with a heart so true
But his life is one of hardship, with no comfort anew
He’s a shepherd, a guardian of the land
But his life is one of struggle, with no helping hand
Oh, shepherd, don’t you see, you’re more than just a name?
You’re a symbol of courage, a heart that beats with honor and fame
You’re a brave man, with a spirit that never fades
A true rustic hero, with a heart that’s made of shades.

Note:- The poem is a tribute to the life of a shepherd, who leads a simple yet challenging life. Despite his bravery and true heart, the shepherd’s life is marked by hardship, toil, and struggle. The poem highlights the contrast between the shepherd’s free-flowing heart and his restrictive life circumstances.

The poem also touches on the theme of identity and recognition. The speaker urges the shepherd to recognize his own worth and value, beyond his mundane daily tasks. The shepherd is portrayed as a symbol of courage, honor, and fame, and his life is celebrated as a testament to his strength and resilience.

Overall, the poem is a poignant and thought-provoking exploration of the human condition, highlighting the complexities and challenges of a simple yet noble life.

27. " Rain and thou "

I was calling out to thou, a desperate plea
But thy imagination left me feeling empty and bare
This restless heart is scaring mine, it's like a warning sign
Erasing your memories, making them seem like a distant lie
Come to me, dear one, like a refreshing rain
I'll cherish every drop, and feel thy love again
In these winds, a strange sensation arises
Maybe it's thy whisper, reaching out to mine eager eyes
Merge with me, dear one, and let our souls unite
Let's become one, and make our love shine bright
Why doth thou haunt mine, dear one, and push me away?
Why do you separate yourself from me, and make me feel lost and grey?
thine body, soul, and essence, I know so well
Why do you make me say, that I'm unaware of your love's spell?
Listen to my cry, dear one, and hear my plea
Don't hurt me so, with your absence's cruel decree
I'm a captive of your love, dear one, with all mine dreams laid low
My heart is lost in your love's delight, with no way to let go.

***Note:-** The poem is a romantic and emotional expression of a person's longing for their loved one. The speaker is desperate to be reunited with their loved one and is calling out to them, begging them to return. The poem explores themes of love, separation, and longing. The speaker remembers the loved one's presence fondly and yearns for their touch and love. They feel lost and grey without their loved one and are desperate to be reunited with them. The poem also touches on the idea of the loved one's imagination and memories. The speaker feels that their loved one's imagination has left them feeling empty and bare, and that their memories are fading away. The tone of the poem is one of desperation, longing, and love. The speaker is pouring their heart out to their loved one, begging them to return and end their emotional pain. The poem is a beautiful expression of the pain of separation and the depth of human love.*

28. " Dove's Letter "

Nowadays , Fie ! Fie ! Shame on thou my beloved
These days now seem like a curse to mine
Day and night, I'm lamenting, searching for thee
Did you receive the letter I sent through my dove?
Why are you angry with me now? Don't ignore me, I implore
Hath mercy on me, and respond to my plea
Are you listening? Don't think I'm unaware of your agony
Did you drink the poison of separation, thinking it was water?
Every moment without you is killing me, oh, how I yearn for you!
My wounds are not healing, please touch them and make them whole
Don't be different from me, don't make me unaware of your love
Don't hurt me with your faithfulness, don't make me feel like I'm dying
Lest your body too wither away in this separation
I'm leaving now, taking my dove with me
Are you building another nest, another love to set me free?
You've made me a ruin, a destroyed and broken soul

My heart is a desert, my love for you, now turned to stone
I'm returning to my nest, my love for you, now lost and cold
My dove, my heart, my everything, now gone, grown old.

Note:- The poem is a heartfelt expression of longing and separation. The speaker is lamenting the loss of their loved one and is searching for them day and night. They are desperate to know if their loved one has received their message and are pleading with them to respond. The speaker is feeling the pain of separation deeply and is begging their loved one to have mercy on them. They are yearning for their loved one's touch and presence, and are feeling like they are dying without them. The poem also touches on the theme of faithfulness and loyalty. The speaker is asking their loved one not to hurt them with their faithfulness and to remember their love for each other. The final stanzas of the poem are a poignant expression of the speaker's despair and loss. They are leaving, taking their heart and soul with them, and are wondering if their loved one is building a new life without them. The poem ends with the speaker's heart turned to stone, their love lost and cold, and their spirit gone, grown old.

29. " Broken:- But Beautiful Soul"

O ! O ! My Gosh , Everyone has broken the strings of my heart
Now I've woven a new melody with my pains
Everyone else got love, but I got wounds and prayers
The outsiders benefited, and even my loved ones did too
Whoever wove hatred into their hearts
Everyone has broken the strings of my heart
They now laugh and pretend to show love and loyalty
They swear by love and faithfulness, but what can be said
About this heartless world where wounds are pelted with stones
Everyone has broken the strings of my heart
I've even folded my hands in solitude
Pain is pain, and even love brings tears
Just like flowers have thorns, now even thorns hurt me
Congratulations to those who got the flowers and left me with the thorns
Everyone has broken the strings of my heart.

Note:- The poem is a heartfelt expression of pain and betrayal. The speaker feels that everyone they trusted has

broken their heart, leaving them with only pain and sorrow. They reflect on how others have found love and happiness, while they have been left with wounds and prayers. The poem also touches on the theme of hypocrisy, where people pretend to show love and loyalty, but ultimately cause harm. The speaker feels that they are living in a heartless world where pain and suffering are inflicted without remorse. The poem concludes with the speaker acknowledging that even love can bring pain, and that they have been left to suffer alone. The final line, "Everyone has broken the strings of my heart," drives home the speaker's sense of despair and abandonment.

30. " Affection's Of Outer Soul "

In this era of Kalyug, love has become a mere formality, where a self-centered lover boasts about their conquests to their beloved, who is smitten by their physical appearance. But is this really what love is all about? Absolutely not! Love is a sacred and sublime bond that transcends physical attraction and is rooted in the depths of the human heart. In today's modern world, love has become a mere game of deception, where people pretend to love each other but are only interested in physical pleasure. The days of true love and loyalty are long gone, and now people are only looking out for their own selfish interests.

My best friend, Mamta Chaturvedi, has been a victim of this kind of love. She fell deeply in love with a self-centered man named Abhishek Tiwari, who only cared about her physical appearance. But when he found someone else who caught his fancy, he dumped Mamta without a second thought.

This kind of love is not only hurtful but also destructive. It leaves the victim feeling broken and betrayed, and it takes a long time to heal from the wounds. Mamta's situation is a classic example of this kind of love. She is still reeling from the shock of Abhishek's betrayal, and it's hard for her to move on.

But I want to tell Mamta that she deserves better. She deserves someone who will love her for who she is, not just for her physical appearance. She deserves someone who will stand by her through thick and thin, and who will never betray her trust.

So, Mamta, don't lose hope. There are still good people out there who will love you for who you are. Don't settle for anyone who doesn't deserve you. You are a beautiful and talented person, and you deserve someone who will appreciate you for all that you are.

"Love is a wonder, a unique thing. It's a deception of the open eyes. Whoever understands it is soaked in the ocean, and the ocean is just a drop."

Note:- The poem is a heartfelt lamentation of the state of love in today's world. The speaker argues that love has become a mere formality, where people are more interested in physical attraction and selfish desires rather than genuine emotions.

The poem cites the example of the speaker's best friend, Mamta Chaturvedi, who was deeply hurt by a self-centered lover named Abhishek Tiwari. Abhishek only cared about Mamta's physical appearance and dumped her when he found someone else who caught his fancy.

The speaker argues that this kind of love is not only hurtful but also destructive. It leaves the victim feeling broken, betrayed, and confused. The speaker emphasizes that true love is a sacred and sublime bond that transcends physical attraction and is rooted in the depths of the human heart. The poem concludes by encouraging Mamta to hold on to hope and not settle for anyone who doesn't deserve her. The speaker reminds Mamta that she deserves someone who will love her for who she is, beyond her physical appearance. The poem ends with a message of resilience and hope, urging Mamta to keep faith in the power of true love.

31. " Eve Shut, Wimin's life Cut"

Fie ! Fie ! Lord , Eve shut ,
Wimin's life cut , Nobody seems brave
Digge'd the eternal hidden cave,
In desolate streets, in empty towns,
A woman wanders, her heart worn down.
With a faded sari, and a heart full of pain,
She searches for solace, but in vain.
Her dreams of palaces, now reduced to dust,
She roams the streets, with a heart that's lost.
No shade, no respite, from the scorching sun,
Her journey is endless, her heart forever undone.
Her body may be weary, but her spirit remains bright,
Like the moon, eclipsed by the darkness of night.
The flowers that once adorned her, now wilted and grey,
Her beauty, lost to the world, fades away.
Memories of her lover, bring a fleeting smile,
But the pain of his absence, makes her heart go the extra mile.
Her footsteps falter, as she wonders why,
Her love, her life, her everything, was reduced to a mere

sigh.
Tears are her only solace, her heart, her only guide,
She weeps, for the love she lost, for the life she could not provide.
She thought she had found love, but it was just a disguise,
For the thorns that pierced her heart, and the pain that opened her eyes.
A mother, with a child in her arms, weeps silently by,
Her tears, a reflection of the pain, that she cannot deny.
The earth, once full of life, now lies barren and still,
A testament to the suffering, that this woman must fulfill.
Her birth, a result of pain, her life, a journey of strife,
Yet, she rises, a phoenix, from the ashes of her life.
But still, she searches, for an answer, for a reprieve,
From the pain, that haunts her, from the sorrow, that she cannot leave.
Where doth a woman's suffering end?
Is it in the desolate streets, or the empty towns she wanders through?
Is it in the pain, that she endures, or the tears, that she sheds anew?
Or is it in the silence, that follows, when her heart, is finally broken in two?

Note:- The poem is a poignant portrayal of a woman's suffering and pain. She wanders alone in desolate streets and empty towns, her heart worn down by the loss of love and the harsh realities of life. Despite her physical and emotional exhaustion, her spirit remains strong, but she is unable to escape the pain that haunts her.

The poem explores themes of love, loss, and the resilience of women in the face of adversity. It highlights the ways in which societal expectations and gender roles can contribute to women's suffering, and the ways in which women are often forced to bear the burden of pain and sacrifice.

Ultimately, the poem asks a powerful and haunting question: "Where does a woman's suffering end?" The answer, of course, is that there is no easy answer, and that women's suffering can take many forms and can be endless.

32. " Thou'rt Not , It's Me "

O ! Gosh that's mine bluff,
She's not mine beloved
Just a Useless Shredded heart,
Who are thou, my first love?
The reason for mine restless heart?
Who are thou, mine first devotion?
The beloved of my dreams?
Who are thou, the idol of deception?
The beat of my heart, the light of my eyes?
Who are you, the missing pages of my book?
You, who abandoned me, leaving me alone in the dark.
I wept, lost and forsaken,
For a moment, I lost myself, and my existence was crushed.
Who played this game, and trampled my soul?
Perhaps it was you, perhaps it was them.
Now, go and leave with him,
This deceitful game, who played it? You?

Note:- The poem is a heartfelt and emotional expression of a person's pain and longing after being abandoned by their first love. The speaker is searching for answers, asking who this person was who captivated their heart and soul. The poem explores themes of love, loss, and deception, with the speaker feeling betrayed and forsaken. The use of rhetorical questions emphasizes the speaker's confusion and emotional turmoil.

Throughout the poem, the speaker grapples with the pain of being left behind, wondering who was responsible for their heartbreak. The final lines, "Now, go and leave with him, This deceitful game, who played it? You?" suggest a sense of resignation and accusation, as the speaker seems to accept that their love is lost, and that their former lover is to blame for the pain they have caused.

33. " Is this love, Or is it Madness "

It's all about the madness , nor love
thou'rt Freaky beloved , just fridge the affection of love,
Is this love, or is it madness that's consuming mine?
A flame that's burning, a passion that's deceiving me.
I'm searching for answers, but they're hard to find,
My heart is racing, my soul is left behind.
Is this love, or is it a cruel joke?
A game of deception, a heart that's about to choke.
The roads are winding, the journey is long,
But I'm walking alone, with a heart that's full of song.
My heartbeat is racing, my pulse is on fire,
My love, my heart, my everything, is a burning desire.
But you're pushing me away, into the dark of night,
Leaving me to die, without a fight.
Is this love, or is it a form of torture?
A slow and painful death, a heart that's about to rupture.
You're saying we'll meet again, in another life,
But for now, I'm left to suffer, and to fight for my life.
Is this love, or is it a cruel and heartless game?
A game of deception, a heart that's about to be tamed.

I'm searching for answers, but they're hard to find,
My heart is breaking, my soul is left behind.

Note:- The poem is a heartfelt and emotional expression of the speaker's confusion and pain in a romantic relationship. The speaker is torn between the intense passion and love they feel, and the hurt and deception they are experiencing.

Throughout the poem, the speaker asks rhetorical questions, wondering if their feelings are truly love or just madness. They describe the pain and suffering they are enduring, feeling like they are being pushed away and left to die.

The poem explores themes of love, heartbreak, deception, and the blurred lines between passion and pain. The speaker's emotions are raw and intense, and the poem conveys a sense of desperation and longing.

Ultimately, the poem concludes with the speaker still searching for answers, their heart breaking, and their soul left behind. The poem is a powerful expression of the complexities and challenges of love and relationships.

34. " Bluff Emotions "

Oh ! My honey , thou've penty emotions
Don't trap mine bluff's lotion
Thine memories have haunted me so much,
That I believed thine deception to be the truth.
thou cheated mine in every way,
Sometimes by telling me stories of love,
And sometimes by showing me the illusion of love.
After a few days, you took everything from me,
Leaving me breathless, like a noose around my neck.
What will you doth now with this lifeless body?
You have already killed the fakir who was drowned in love.
Don't torture mine soul now,
Don't try to justify thine deception as love.
Leave me alone, and let me go.
Take your leave from the world of my dreams,
And go your own way, somewhere else.
But have mercy on me, and spare others too,
Not everyone can bear the weight of your deception.
And if you truly love someone,
That would be the greatest deception of all.

Note:- The poem is a heartfelt and emotional expression of the speaker's pain and betrayal in a romantic relationship. The speaker feels haunted by the memories of their loved one, who deceived and cheated them in every way. The poem describes how the speaker was manipulated and lied to, with the loved one using stories of love and illusions of affection to control and exploit them. The speaker feels like they have been left breathless and lifeless, with their soul crushed by the weight of the deception. The poem is a plea for the loved one to leave the speaker alone and to spare others from their deception. The speaker warns that not everyone can bear the weight of their loved one's deception, and that if they truly love someone, it would be the greatest deception of all. Overall, the poem is a powerful expression of the pain and betrayal that can occur in romantic relationships, and the importance of recognizing and escaping from toxic and deceptive relationships.

35. " Depth Of Love "

O, My Darling thou'rt , hath great depth of love
Why didst you afraid, my love, of the world's cruelty?
I am here, don't you know?
Why are thou burning in the darkness of deception?
I am here, don't you know?
Why are you worried about something that's not worth it?
I am here, don't you know?
I will take you far away, to a city of light,
Where your feet will not stumble, and you will not be hurt.
Why are you afraid, my love? I am here.
We were just beginning to write our love story,
And you're already planning your escape.
Have I loved you any less? Why are you drifting away from me?
Don't go, my love. I am here.
I promise to be with you till the end of time,
To be your companion, your friend, your love.
Why are you worried about deception? I am here.
Come, let's get lost in the whirlpool of love,
And forget about life and death.
Who are you searching for in this whirlpool?
There's no one, but I am here.

What are you saying, my love? You're drifting away from me,
And yet, I'm still commanding you to love me.
There's no one left on this earth, but I am here.
Don't you know, my love, I am here?

Note:- The poem is a heartfelt and emotional expression of the speaker's love and devotion to their beloved. The speaker is trying to reassure their loved one that they have nothing to fear, as they are there to protect and care for them.

The poem explores themes of love, fear, deception, and devotion. The speaker promises to take their loved one away from the darkness of deception and to a place of safety and love. They ask their loved one why they are drifting away from them, and reassure them that they will always be there for them.

The poem also touches on the idea of the whirlpool of love, where the speaker invites their loved one to get lost with them and forget about the worries of life and death. The poem ends with the speaker reaffirming their presence and devotion to their loved one, and asking them to remember that they are always there for them.

36. " Murk Of Stuff "

Fie ! Fie Lord , Got the murk of love ,
It's been a heap of love stuff,
Leave thine home and come to see,
A traveler has arrived, a lover of sorrow.
Perhaps they've brought their heart, freed from pain,
And are searching for you, don't let them leave in vain.
Don't let them wander, searching for you,
Acknowledge your love, and set aside your deception.
Lest the traveler return, and get lost in their wounds,
And disappear in the alleys of deceit.
Oh, traveler, you look so worn out,
Perhaps you're the one she's been searching for.
Make yourself known, lest you get lost,
In the alleys of deception, and forget your way.
My love, how can you deny,
The one you've recognized, and yet claim you don't know?
What kind of love is this, that doesn't listen,
Our traveler has gotten lost, in your streets, and has fallen asleep.
Perhaps they won't return, the traveler may be lost,
Go and meet them, oh lover, lest they disappear.
You've come, even if only for a moment,

And brought solace to my broken heart.

Note:- The poem is a beautiful and emotional expression of love, longing, and heartache. The speaker is addressing a loved one, asking them to leave their home and come to see a traveler who has arrived, searching for them.

The poem explores themes of love, deception, and heartache, as the speaker warns the loved one not to let the traveler leave in vain, and to acknowledge their love and set aside their deception.

The poem also touches on the idea of the traveler being worn out and lost, and the speaker's concern that they may disappear if not found. The poem ends with the speaker expressing gratitude for the traveler's brief visit, which brought solace to their broken heart.

Overall, the poem is a poignant and emotional expression of the complexities of love and relationships, and the longing and heartache that can accompany them.

37. " Queer Affection "

O, Gosh I'm unable to express mine feelings for her
Don't Stretched the love of stir,
Now that I've gotten to know thou,
I've made a connection with thou,
Mine heart is feeling something new.
Even the sky is telling me to connect with thou,
But mine love is a deception, a blood-soaked game.
Yet, I'm still worried about thine well-being.
Come back to the same place where we first met,
Don't thou remember where you first captured my heart?
Where you began the process of completing my heart,
And where you pierced my wounded heart with yours.

Note:- The poem is a heartfelt expression of love and longing. The speaker has formed a connection with someone and is feeling a new sensation in their heart. Despite being aware that their love is a deception and a painful game, they are still concerned about the well-being of the person they love.

The speaker invites the person to return to the place where they first met, where their heart was captured and completed. The poem is a nostalgic and emotional appeal to rekindle the love and connection that was once shared.

The speaker's words are a poignant expression of the complexities and challenges of love.

38. " Aww ! When I Met her "

Ah ! My Gosh Nowadays
Days are passing by, and I'm just lost in gazing at thou,
I have no other task or purpose, but to see thou.
Morning and evening, I yearn for thine sight,
And I have no other occupation, but to behold thou.
When night falls, I remember thou, and gaze at thine face,
In a single moment, I see the deception of thee love.
Whenever I stand in front of the mirror,
My reflection says, "Come, let's gaze at your beloved."
I don't know what magic your love possesses,
But every time, my reflection tells me to kiss the mirror.
Now, whenever I look up at the sky,
I see your face everywhere.
I even see your face in the moon,
And the stars seem scattered, yet they form your image.
I wonder how they can create your picture,
Despite being scattered and disjointed.
Now, your memory has grown so strong,
That my heartbeats have begun to slow down.
Perhaps now, even death wants to take me away,

To the heavens, to the afterlife.
I've searched every corner of the world,
And now, I'm left with no place to go.
I'm heading towards mine grave, carrying thine memory,
If our love is true, come to mine grave.

Note:- The poem is a heartfelt expression of love and longing. The speaker is completely consumed by their love for the beloved and spends every waking moment thinking of them. They see the beloved's face everywhere, even in the stars and the moon.

The speaker's love has become so strong that it's affecting their heartbeats, and they feel like they're being pulled towards death. They've searched the entire world for the beloved, but now they're left with nowhere to go.

The poem ends with the speaker asking the beloved to come to their grave if their love is true. The poem is a beautiful expression of the all-consuming nature of love and the way it can transcend even death.

39. " Life's Mistake:- Bluff

O , Thou'rt like Bluff of Life
Mine heart felt, thine eyes intoxicated
Whose fainted mine Soul, Sight,
Falling in love with thou, mine heart's first mistake,
Admitting my love, my life's biggest heartache.
People celebrate love with joy and delight,
But I, a lover, wander the footpaths, lost in night.
I had no refuge, no place to call mine own,
So I left everything, and now the footpath is my home.
I didn't know that loving you would lead to my demise,
That it would destroy me, and leave me with a lifetime of sighs.
I thought your love would bring me wealth, fame, and prestige,
But instead, it led me to the graveyard, where my heart would rest in peace.
I thought you'd help me build a new world, a new life,
But instead, you left me with nothing, but a broken heart, and a strife.

Your walk, your style, it fooled me every time,
You're the only one, who made me feel so blind.
You've ruined me, destroyed me, left me with nothing to say,
Now leave this city, and go away.
I'll stay on the footpath, it's where I belong,
A place where love has left me, with a heart that's turned to stone.

Note:- The poem is a heart-wrenching expression of love, loss, and betrayal. The speaker reflects on how falling in love with the person they address was their biggest mistake, and admitting their love was their life's biggest heartache.

The poem explores the contrast between how others celebrate love and how the speaker's love has led to their downfall. The speaker is left with nothing, wandering the footpaths, and feeling lost and alone.

The poem also touches on the theme of deception, as the speaker feels they were fooled by the person they loved. The speaker's heart has been broken, and they are left with nothing but a lifetime of sighs and a heart that has turned to stone.

The poem ends with the speaker asking the person they loved to leave the city, and for them to stay on the footpath, which has become their home.

40. " Thine Fake Affection "

Shame on the new bond, may joy be with thou,
I've forgiven you, erased thine deceit from mine memories.
Take the hand of that deception, and depart to thine realm of fraud,
Just show mercy on that body of deception, don't feign love.
Don't pretend to love, don't show affection,
If need be, reveal your deception to that person too.
Do as you've done, however thou've done,
Now leave from here, or they will leave too,
Saying "I gave mine heart, but they abandoned me,
Cutting off my support in the midst of oure journey."

***Note:-** The poem is a farewell address to a former lover who has been unfaithful. The speaker congratulates the ex-lover on their new relationship and announces that they have forgiven them and erased the memories of their deceit.*

The speaker tells the ex-lover to leave and go to their own world of fraud, but asks them to show mercy on the person they deceived (likely referring to themselves). The speaker warns the ex-lover not to pretend to love or show affection

if they don't mean it.
The poem ends with a warning that if the ex-lover doesn't leave, the other person will eventually leave too, and will say that they gave their heart but were abandoned and had their support cut off in the middle of their journey. the poem is about closure, forgiveness, and warning an ex-lover to be honest in their future relationships.

41. " Duh ! My bluff's Affection "

Duh ! My Honey thine bluff love ,
Cut mine into shredded par,
"Come, let us teach thou love's sweet way,
And guide thou through the river's flow, to a brighter day.
We'll show thou how to love, to cherish and adore,
And heal the wounds that you've endured, forevermore.
No matter if you've been unfaithful, we'll transform thine heart,
And mold you into a work of art, a brand new start.
My wounds still linger, but I'll be thine balm,
Healing thine pain, soothing thine calm.
Acknowledge mine sorrow, share mine grief,
Or thine tears will be but a mere relief.
In your whirlpool of love, I'll gladly drown,
And find solace in thine embrace, mine heart's sweet crown.
If thou hesitate, don't worry, we'll give thou a chance,
Even the ungrateful will find a second dance.
We'll adorn thou with beauty, inside and out,
And teach you love's true meaning, without a doubt.

So come with me, let's walk this path together,
And discover love's true beauty, in every weather."

Note:- The poem is a heartfelt and passionate invitation to someone to learn about love and relationships. The speaker offers to guide the person through the challenges of love and help them heal from past wounds. The poem promises transformation, redemption, and a new start, even for those who have been unfaithful.

The speaker shares their own vulnerability, acknowledging that their wounds still linger, but they are willing to be a source of comfort and healing for the other person. The poem encourages the person to acknowledge and share in the speaker's sorrow, and warns that insincere tears will not be enough.

The poem also expresses a willingness to embrace the whirlpool of love and find solace in the other person's embrace. It offers a second chance to those who have been ungrateful and promises to adorn them with inner and outer beauty.

Ultimately, the poem invites the person to walk the path of love together, exploring its true meaning and beauty in all circumstances. The tone is one of hope, redemption, and the promise of new beginnings.

42. " Wimin's Charm "

Ah ! Mine Affection for her,
Day by day , I'm unhold the charm of thy soul,
"Ages ago, love's intoxication began to unfold,
But why didst deception's haze start to hold?
Everyone's trapped in deceit's sway,
I ask about their state, but they just say,
"Mine heart's deceived, what can I do?"
Tell me, what's happened to thine heart?
Listen to the tale of that unfaithful one,
Deception's the game, and hearts are undone.
What joy didst thou find in this deceitful night?
From dawn till dusk, colors of love took flight.
Why did this happen? Was it a cruel fate?
thou've wounded hearts, and now it's too late.
Leave thine tricks and deceitful ways,
And follow the path of love's genuine sway.
Heal these broken hearts, and mend their pain,
For in love's true embrace, they'll find their gain.
No more deception, no more heartache's might,
Just love's pure solace, shining like a light."

Note:- The poem explores the theme of love, deception, and heartbreak. It begins by questioning how deception crept

into love's intoxication and trapped everyone in its sway. The speaker asks about the state of others' hearts, but they just say they're deceived and don't know what to do.
The poem then tells the tale of an unfaithful person who played the game of deception, causing hearts to be undone. It asks what joy was found in that deceitful night, when love's colors took flight from dawn till dusk.
The poem expresses sorrow and regret, wondering why this happened and if it was a cruel fate. It acknowledges the wounded hearts and the lateness of the hour.
Finally, the poem urges the listener to leave their deceitful ways and follow the genuine path of love. It encourages healing and mending the pain of broken hearts, promising that in love's true embrace, they'll find their gain. The poem concludes by renouncing deception and heartache, and embracing love's pure solace and light.

43. “ Beloved's Voice ”

It’s been ages since I heard your melody,
Now my heart yearns to hear your symphony.
After a long wait, I’ve been imagining,
But I’ve forgotten the tune, it’s been so long since hearing.
Perhaps you haven’t forgotten, come and remind,
Let’s put the past behind, I’ve forgiven in kind.
Oh, reconnect with me, and soothe my soul,
Heal my wounds with love’s balm, and make me whole.

Theme:-

The poem explores the themes of nostalgia, forgiveness, and the desire for reconnection in a relationship.

Structure:-

The poem consists of six stanzas, each with a rhyme scheme that adds to the musical quality of the verse. The structure is well-balanced, with each stanza contributing to the overall narrative.

Tone:-

The tone of the poem is melancholic, yet hopeful. The speaker expresses a deep sense of longing and yearning, but also conveys a willingness to forgive and move forward.

Imagery and Metaphor:-

The poem employs vivid imagery and metaphor to convey the speaker's emotions. For example, the comparison of the beloved's voice to a "melody" and a "symphony" creates a powerful musical metaphor that underscores the speaker's deep emotional connection to the beloved.

Emotional Journey:-

The poem takes the reader on an emotional journey, from the pain of separation to the hope of reconciliation. The speaker's emotions are deeply personal and relatable, making the poem a powerful expression of universal human feelings.

44. " Duh ! It's thine hallucinations "

Ah ! Mine love for her increasing moment by moment,
But thou've potential to cheated like bloomy eyes,
Duh ! Mine Soul numb,
This heart is yearning for thou, like a thirsty person yearns for water.
Come back to mine, and fill the deep wound in mine world.
Don't torture me so much that my life slips away.
Now, please come back, and accept my words.
Even my desires seem incomplete without thou.
How many times can I imagine thou?
This intoxication of love is overwhelming me so much that my sorrow is not decreasing,
only pain, wounds, and restlessness are surrounding mine,
and the wind of separation is blowing everywhere.

Note:- The poem is a heartfelt expression of longing and yearning for a loved one. The speaker's heart is filled with a deep emotional pain, and they implore their beloved to return to them. The poem describes the intensity of the speaker's love and the overwhelming sorrow they feel in the absence of their beloved. The speaker's desires and imagination are consumed by thoughts of their loved one, and they feel incomplete without them. The poem is a poignant expression of the pain of separation and the all-consuming nature of love.

45. "Fie ! Mine Age sudden counting down like stair"

Fie ! Mine Age sudden counting down like stair,
Stop thine hallucinations , give mine healthy age fair,
Mine life is fading away, waiting for thou,
Even patience is heading towards the grave, too.
I'm slowly laying to rest mine heart, mine breath,
And your memories, one by one, in death.
Before I turn into a coffin's box,
Come, take my soul, and hold it close.
Forget your deception, and the pain thou've caused,
For years have passed without thou, and mine heart is paused.
Seasonless rains have fallen, and I've grown old,
My life, too, has faded, like the seasons cold.
In this quiet grave, there's no unfulfilled desire,
Only the stillness of death, my heart's final fire.

Note:- The poem is a poignant expression of longing and separation. The speaker's life is fading away as they wait for their beloved, and even their patience is dwindling.

The speaker is slowly letting go of their heart, breath, and memories, and is preparing for death.

The poem is a desperate plea to the beloved to return and take the speaker's soul before it's too late. The speaker asks the beloved to forget their past deceptions and the pain they caused, and to come back to them.

The poem also reflects on the passing of time and the speaker's growing old. The speaker's life has faded away, and they are left with no unfulfilled desires, only the stillness of death. The poem ends with the image of the speaker's heart's final flame being extinguished.

46. " Nor happiness, Nor Bluff "

Ah ! Mine days seems like complex , nor happiness
Thine soul interact with mine like , either bluff sadness
Don't torture mine so much that my life slips away,
thou're not just a breeze that can take mine breath away.
Mine heartbeats are not just a mere mortal sound,
If they stop, my life will fade, and I'll be lost, unfound.
thou're not a Laila, a love that's true and kind,
Just a deceiver, a heart that's left behind.
thou're not a reflection of truth, a mirror to the soul,
If thou don't reveal the truth, people will be consumed by deceit's dark role.
Go, lose yourself in thine dreams of fidelity,
But thou're just a deceiver, a queen of love's duplicity.
thou're not a monarch, a ruler of the heart,
Just a charlatan, a weaver of love's torn apart.
Thine beauty is a snare, a trap that's hard to define,
thou're a storm that sweeps away memories, leaving heart and mind entwined.
thou're a faithless one, a heart that's cold as stone,
thou deceive and betray, leaving hearts to atone.

thou come and go, a fleeting love, a moment's pleasure,
But thine deception leaves a scar, a heart that's lost its treasure.

Note:- The poem is a lamentation of a love that has turned sour. The speaker expresses their emotional pain and suffering, feeling that their life is slipping away due to the beloved's deception and betrayal.

The poem accuses the beloved of being a deceiver, a charlatan, and a faithless one, who has swept away memories and left the speaker's heart and mind entwined in pain.

The speaker feels that the beloved's beauty is a trap, a snare that is hard to define, and that their love is a fleeting pleasure that leaves a scar and a heart that's lost its treasure.

The poem is a powerful expression of the pain and suffering that can result from a love that has turned toxic and deceptive. It is a cry of anguish and a plea for the beloved to reveal the truth and end the deception

www.ingramcontent.com/pod-product-compliance
Lightning Source LLC
LaVergne TN
LVHW041116150826
845673LV00007B/2070

* 9 7 9 8 8 9 6 3 2 5 0 2 4 *